TRANZLATY

Language is for everyone
语言属于每个人

Aladdin and the Wonderful Lamp

阿拉丁与奇妙的灯

Antoine Galland

安托万·加兰

English / 普通话

Copyright © 2025 Tranzlaty
All rights reserved
Published by Tranzlaty
ISBN: 978-1-83566-915-0
Original text by Antoine Galland
From *"Les mille et une nuits"*
First published in French in 1704
Taken from The Blue Fairy Book
Collected and translated by Andrew Lang
www.tranzlaty.com

Once upon a time there lived a poor tailor
从前，有一个穷裁缝
this poor tailor had a son called Aladdin
这个可怜的裁缝有一个儿子叫阿拉丁
Aladdin was a careless, idle boy who did nothing
阿拉丁是一个粗心大意、懒惰的男孩，他什么也不做
although, he did like to play ball all day long
尽管他确实喜欢整天打球
this he did in the streets with other little idle boys
他在街上和其他无所事事的小男孩一起做这件事
This so grieved the father that he died
父亲因此悲痛欲绝，最终去世
his mother cried and prayed, but nothing helped
他的母亲哭泣并祈祷，但毫无作用
despite her pleading, Aladdin did not mend his ways
尽管她恳求，阿拉丁还是没有改过自新
One day, Aladdin was playing in the streets, as usual
有一天，阿拉丁像往常一样在街上玩耍
a stranger asked him his age
一个陌生人问他年龄
and he asked him, "are you not the son of Mustapha the tailor?"
他问他："你不是裁缝穆斯塔法的儿子吗？"
"I am the son of Mustapha, sir," replied Aladdin
阿拉丁回答："我是穆斯塔法的儿子，先生。"
"but he died a long time ago"
"但他很久以前就去世了"
the stranger was a famous African magician
这位陌生人是一位著名的非洲魔术师
and he fell on his neck and kissed him
然后他抱着他的脖子，亲吻他
"I am your uncle," said the magician
魔术师说："我是你叔叔。"
"I knew you from your likeness to my brother"

"我认识你,因为你和我哥哥很像"
"Go to your mother and tell her I am coming"
"去找你妈妈,告诉她我来了"
Aladdin ran home and told his mother of his newly found uncle
阿拉丁跑回家告诉妈妈他新找到了一个叔叔
"Indeed, child," she said, "your father had a brother"
"孩子,你爸爸确实有一个兄弟。"
"but I always thought he was dead"
"但我一直以为他死了"
However, she prepared supper for the visitor
不过,她为来访者准备了晚餐
and she bade Aladdin to seek his uncle
她叫阿拉丁去找他的叔叔
Aladdin's uncle came laden with wine and fruit
阿拉丁的叔叔带着酒和水果来了
He fell down and kissed the place where Mustapha used to sit
他倒下并亲吻了穆斯塔法曾经坐过的地方
and he bid Aladdin's mother not to be surprised
他告诉阿拉丁的母亲不要惊讶
he explained he had been out of the country for forty years
他解释说他已经出国四十年了
He then turned to Aladdin and asked him his trade
然后他转向阿拉丁,问他做什么生意
but the boy hung his head in shame
但男孩羞愧地低下了头
and his mother burst into tears
他的母亲大哭起来
so Aladdin's uncle offered to provide food
于是阿拉丁的叔叔主动提出提供食物
The next day he bought Aladdin a fine set of clothes
第二天,他给阿拉丁买了一套漂亮的衣服
and he took him all over the city

他带他走遍了整个城市
he showed him the sights of the city
他向他展示了这座城市的风景
at nightfall he brought him home to his mother
夜幕降临，他把他带回家交给母亲
his mother was overjoyed to see her son so well dressed
母亲看到儿子穿得这么好，欣喜若狂
The next day the magician led Aladdin into some beautiful gardens
第二天，魔术师带阿拉丁去了一些美丽的花园
this was a long way outside the city gates
距离城门很远
They sat down by a fountain
他们坐在喷泉边
and the magician pulled a cake from his girdle
魔术师从腰带里拿出一块蛋糕
he divided the cake between the two of them
他把蛋糕分给了他们两个
Then they journeyed onward till they almost reached the mountains
然后他们继续前行，直到快到达山上
Aladdin was so tired that he begged to go back
阿拉丁太累了，他恳求回去
but the magician beguiled him with pleasant stories
但魔术师用有趣的故事迷惑了他
and he led him on in spite of his laziness
尽管他很懒，他还是引导他
At last they came to two mountains
最后他们来到两座山前
the two mountains were divided by a narrow valley
两座山被一道狭窄的山谷分开
"We will go no farther," said the false uncle
"我们不再往前走了。"假叔叔说。
"I will show you something wonderful"

"我会让你看一些奇妙的东西"
"gather up sticks, while I kindle a fire"
"收集好木棍,我来点火"
When the fire was lit the magician threw a powder on it
当火被点燃时,魔术师往火上撒了粉末
and he said some magical words
他说了一些神奇的话
The earth trembled a little and opened in front of them
大地微微颤动,在他们面前裂开
a square flat stone revealed itself
一块方形扁平的石头显露出来
and in the middle of the stone was a brass ring
石头中间有一个铜环
Aladdin tried to run away
阿拉丁试图逃跑
but the magician caught him
但魔术师抓住了他
and gave him a blow that knocked him down
并给了他一拳,把他打倒在地
"What have I done, uncle?" he said, piteously
"我做了什么,叔叔?"他可怜兮兮地说。
the magician said more kindly, "Fear nothing, but obey me"
魔术师则温和地说道:"别怕,只要听我的。"
"Beneath this stone lies a treasure which is to be yours"
"这块石头下面隐藏着属于你的宝藏"
"and no one else may touch this treasure"
"其他任何人都不可以触碰这个宝藏"
"so you must do exactly as I tell you"
"所以你必须完全按照我告诉你的去做"
At the mention of treasure Aladdin forgot his fears
一提到宝藏,阿拉丁就忘记了他的恐惧
he grasped the ring as he was told
他按照吩咐抓住了戒指
and he said the names of his father and grandfather

他说出了他父亲和祖父的名字
The stone came up quite easily
石头很容易就被取了上来
and some steps appeared in front of them
他们面前出现了一些台阶
"Go down," said the magician
魔术师说："下去吧。"
"at the foot of those steps you will find an open door"
"在这些台阶下，你会发现一扇敞开的门"
"the door leads into three large halls"
"这扇门通向三个大厅"
"Tuck up your gown and go through the halls"
"卷起你的长袍，穿过大厅"
"make sure not to touch anything"
"确保不要碰到任何东西"
"if you touch anything, you will instantly die"
"如果你触碰任何东西，你就会立即死亡"
"These halls lead into a garden of fine fruit trees"
"这些大厅通向一个种满美丽果树的花园"
"Walk on until you reach a gap in the terrace"
"一直走，直到到达露台的空隙"
"there you will see a lighted lamp"
"在那里你会看到一盏亮着的灯"
"Pour out the oil of the lamp"
"倒掉灯里的油"
"and then bring me the lamp"
"然后把灯给我拿来"
He drew a ring from his finger and gave it to Aladdin
他从手指上取下一枚戒指，交给了阿拉丁
and he bid him to prosper
他祝愿他兴旺发达
Aladdin found everything as the magician had said
阿拉丁正如魔术师所说的那样找到了一切
he gathered some fruit off the trees

他从树上摘了一些水果
and, having got the lamp, he arrived at the mouth of the cave
他拿着灯,来到洞口
The magician cried out in a great hurry
魔术师急忙喊道
"Make haste and give me the lamp"
"快把灯给我"
Aladdin refused to do this until he was out of the cave
阿拉丁拒绝这样做,直到他走出洞穴
The magician flew into a terrible rage
魔术师勃然大怒
he threw some more powder on to the fire
他又往火里扔了一些火粉
and then he cast another magic spell
然后他又施了一个魔法
and the stone rolled back into its place
石头滚回原处
The magician left Persia for ever
魔术师永远离开了波斯
this plainly showed that he was no uncle of Aladdin's
这清楚地表明他不是阿拉丁的叔叔
what he really was was a cunning magician
他其实是一个狡猾的魔术师
a magician who had read of a magic lamp
读过有关神灯的魔术师
a magic lamp which would make him the most powerful man in the world
一盏能让他成为世界上最有权势的人的神灯
but he alone knew where to find the magic lamp
但只有他知道在哪里可以找到神灯
and he could only receive the magic lamp from the hand of another
他只能从别人手中接过神灯
He had picked out the foolish Aladdin for this purpose

他为此特意挑选了愚蠢的阿拉丁
he had intended to get the magical lamp and kill him afterwards
他原本打算拿到神灯然后杀了他
For two days Aladdin remained in the dark
阿拉丁在黑暗中呆了两天
he cried and lamented his situation
他哭着哀叹自己的处境
At last he clasped his hands in prayer
最后他双手合十祈祷
and in so doing he rubbed the ring
他这样做是为了摩擦戒指
the magician had forgotten to take the ring back from him
魔术师忘记把戒指拿回来了
Immediately an enormous and frightful genie rose out of the earth
立刻，一个巨大而可怕的妖怪从地上冒了出来
"What would thou have me do?"
"你想让我做什么？"
"I am the Slave of the Ring"
"我是魔戒的奴隶"
"and I will obey thee in all things"
"我将在一切事上顺服你"
Aladdin fearlessly replied: "Deliver me from this place!"
阿拉丁勇敢地回答道："救我离开这个地方！"
and the earth opened above him
大地在他上面裂开了
and he found himself outside
他发现自己身处外面
As soon as his eyes could bear the light he went home
一旦他的眼睛能忍受光线，他就回家了
but he fainted when he got there
但到达那里后他晕倒了
When he came to himself he told his mother what had

happened
当他清醒过来后,他告诉母亲所发生的事
and he showed her the lamp
他给她看了那盏灯
and he showed her the fruits he had gathered in the garden
他向她展示了他在花园里采摘的水果
the fruits were, in reality, precious stones
这些水果实际上是宝石
He then asked for some food
然后他要了一些食物
"Alas! child," she said
"哎呀!孩子," 她说。
"I have no food in the house"
"我家里没有食物了"
"but I have spun a little cotton"
"但我纺了一点棉花"
"and I will go and sell the cotton"
"我要去卖棉花"
Aladdin bade her keep her cotton
阿拉丁吩咐她把棉花收起来
he told her he would sell the magic lamp instead of the cotton
他告诉她,他要卖的是神灯,而不是棉花
As it was very dirty she began to rub the magic lamp
由于它很脏,她开始擦拭神灯
a clean magic lamp might fetch a higher price
干净的魔灯可能会卖出更高的价格
Instantly a hideous genie appeared
立刻出现了一个丑陋的精灵
he asked what she would like to have
他问她想要什么
at the sight of the genie she fainted
一看见精灵她就晕倒了
but Aladdin, snatching the magic lamp, said boldly:

阿拉丁一把夺过神灯，大胆地说：
"Fetch me something to eat!"
"给我拿点吃的来！"
The genie returned with a silver bowl
精灵带着一个银碗回来了
he had twelve silver plates containing rich meats
他有十二个银盘子，里面盛着丰富的肉
and he had two silver cups and two bottles of wine
他有两个银杯和两瓶酒
Aladdin's mother, when she came to herself, said:
阿拉丁的母亲清醒过来后说道：
"Whence comes this splendid feast?"
"这么丰盛的宴席是从哪里来的？"
"Ask not where this food came from, but eat, mother," replied Aladdin
阿拉丁回答说："不要问这些食物是从哪里来的，妈妈，吃吧。"
So they sat at breakfast till it was dinner-time
于是他们坐在一起吃早餐，直到晚餐时间
and Aladdin told his mother about the magic lamp
阿拉丁告诉妈妈关于神灯的事
She begged him to sell the magic lamp
她求他卖掉神灯
"let us have nothing to do with devils"
"让我们不要和魔鬼有任何关系"
but Aladdin had thought it would be wiser to use the magic lamp
但阿拉丁认为使用神灯更明智
"chance hath made us aware of the magic lamp's virtues"
"偶然的机会让我们意识到了神灯的功效"
"we will use the magic lamp, and we will use the ring"
"我们会用到魔法灯，也会用到戒指"
"I shall always wear the ring on my finger"
"我会永远戴着戒指"

When they had eaten all the genie had brought, Aladdin sold one of the silver plates
当他们吃完神灵带来的所有食物后,阿拉丁卖掉了其中一个银盘
and when he needed money again he sold the next plate
当他再次需要钱时,他就卖掉了下一盘
he did this until no plates were left
一直到没有盘子为止
He then made another wish to the genie
然后他又向精灵许了另一个愿望
and the genie gave him another set of plates
精灵又给了他一副盘子
and in this way they lived for many years
他们就这样生活了很多年
One day Aladdin heard an order from the Sultan
有一天,阿拉丁听到了苏丹的命令
everyone was to stay at home and close their shutters
每个人都呆在家里,关上百叶窗
the Princess was going to and from her bath
公主正要去洗澡
Aladdin was seized by a desire to see her face
阿拉丁渴望看到她的脸
although it was very difficult to see her face
尽管很难看清她的脸
because everywhere she went she wore a veil
因为她无论去哪里都戴着面纱
He hid himself behind the door of the bath
他躲在浴室门后面
and he peeped through a chink in the door
他从门缝里往外看
The Princess lifted her veil as she went in to the bath
公主走进浴室时掀起了面纱
and she looked so beautiful that Aladdin instantly fell in love with her

她看起来如此美丽,阿拉丁立刻爱上了她
He went home so changed that his mother was frightened
他回家后变了样,他妈妈都吓坏了
He told her he loved the Princess so deeply that he could not live without her
他告诉她,他深爱着公主,没有她他就活不下去。
and he wanted to ask her in marriage of her father
他想向她的父亲求婚
His mother, on hearing this, burst out laughing
他妈妈听到这话,哈哈大笑起来
but Aladdin finally convinced her to go to the Sultan
但阿拉丁最终说服她去见苏丹
and she was going to carry his request
她将履行他的请求
She fetched a napkin and laid in it the magic fruits
她拿来一张餐巾纸,把魔法水果放在里面
the magic fruits from the enchanted garden
魔法花园里的魔法水果
the fruits sparkled and shone like the most beautiful jewels
水果闪闪发光,就像最美丽的珠宝
She took the magic fruits with her to please the Sultan
她带着魔法果实去取悦苏丹
and she set out, trusting in the lamp
她出发了,相信灯
The Grand Vizier and the lords of council had just gone into the palace
大维齐尔和枢密院议员们刚刚进入宫殿
and she placed herself in front of the Sultan
她站在苏丹面前
He, however, took no notice of her
但他没有理会她
She went every day for a week
她连续一周每天都去
and she stood in the same place

她站在同一个地方
When the council broke up on the sixth day the Sultan said to his Vizier:
第六天会议结束时,苏丹对宰相说:
"I see a certain woman in the audience-chamber every day"
"我每天都会在觐见厅里看到一个女人"
"she is always carrying something in a napkin"
"她总是用餐巾纸拿着东西"
"Call her to come to us, next time"
"下次叫她来我们这里"
"so that I may find out what she wants"
"这样我就能知道她想要什么"
Next day the Vizier gave her a sign
第二天,宰相给了她一个信号
she went up to the foot of the throne
她走到王座脚下
and she remained kneeling till the Sultan spoke to her
她一直跪着,直到苏丹对她说话
"Rise, good woman, tell me what you want"
"起来,好女人,告诉我你想要什么"
She hesitated, so the Sultan sent away all but the Vizier
她犹豫了,于是苏丹把所有人都打发走了,只留下了宰相
and he bade her to speak frankly
他让她坦白说
and he promised to forgive her for anything she might say
他答应原谅她说的任何话
She then told him of her son's great love for the Princess
然后她告诉他她儿子对公主的深爱
"I prayed for him to forget her," she said
她说:"我祈祷他忘了她。"
"but my prayers were in vain"
"但我的祈祷徒劳无功"
"he threatened to do some desperate deed if I refused to go"

"他威胁说,如果我拒绝去,他就会采取一些极端行动"

"and so I ask your Majesty for the hand of the Princess"
"因此我请求陛下娶公主为妻。"

"but now I pray you to forgive me"
"但现在我请求你原谅我"

"and I pray that you forgive my son Aladdin"
"我祈求您原谅我的儿子阿拉丁"

The Sultan asked her kindly what she had in the napkin
苏丹亲切地问她餐巾里有什么

so she unfolded the napkin
于是她打开了餐巾

and she presented the jewels to the Sultan
她把珠宝献给了苏丹

He was thunderstruck by the beauty of the jewels
他被这些珠宝的美丽惊呆了

and he turned to the Vizier and asked, "What sayest thou?"
他转身问宰相:"你说什么?"

"Ought I not to bestow the Princess on one who values her at such a price?"
"我难道不应该把公主赐给一个如此珍视她的人吗?"

The Vizier wanted her for his own son
宰相想让她成为自己的儿子

so he begged the Sultan to withhold her for three months
于是他请求苏丹扣留她三个月

perhaps within the time his son would contrive to make a richer present
也许在他儿子想出更丰盛的礼物的时候

The Sultan granted the wish of his Vizier
苏丹满足了维齐尔的愿望

and he told Aladdin's mother that he consented to the marriage
他告诉阿拉丁的母亲他同意这桩婚事

but she was not allowed appear before him again for three months
但三个月内她不被允许再次出现在他面前
Aladdin waited patiently for nearly three months
阿拉丁耐心等待了近三个月
after two months had elapsed his mother went to go to the market
两个月后,他妈妈去市场
she was going into the city to buy oil
她要进城买油
when she got to the market she found every one rejoicing
当她到达市场时,她发现每个人都很高兴
so she asked what was going on
于是她问发生了什么事
"Do you not know?" was the answer
"你不知道吗?"
"the son of the Grand Vizier is to marry the Sultan's daughter tonight"
"大维齐尔的儿子今晚要娶苏丹的女儿"
Breathless, she ran and told Aladdin
她气喘吁吁地跑去告诉阿拉丁
at first Aladdin was overwhelmed
一开始阿拉丁不知所措
but then he thought of the magic lamp and rubbed it
但后来他想到了神灯,就擦了一下
once again the genie appeared out of the lamp
神灯里又出现了一次
"What is thy will?" asked the genie
"你的旨意是什么?" 妖怪问
"The Sultan, as thou knowest, has broken his promise to me"
"如你所知,苏丹违背了对我的诺言。"
"the Vizier's son is to have the Princess"
"宰相的儿子将拥有公主"
"My command is that tonight you bring the bride and bridegroom"

"我的命令是，今晚你必须带新娘和新郎来"
"Master, I obey," said the genie
"主人，我遵命。"精灵说道
Aladdin then went to his chamber
然后阿拉丁回到了他的房间
sure enough, at midnight the genie transported a bed
果然，半夜时分，精灵运来了一张床
and the bed contained the Vizier's son and the Princess
床上躺着宰相的儿子和公主
"Take this new-married man, genie," he said
他说："精灵，带上这个新婚男人吧。"
"put him outside in the cold for the night"
"把他放在外面寒冷的地方过夜"
"then return the couple again at daybreak"
"然后在黎明时分将他们送回。"
So the genie took the Vizier's son out of bed
于是精灵把宰相的儿子从床上带了下来
and he left Aladdin with the Princess
他把阿拉丁留给了公主
"Fear nothing," Aladdin said to her, "you are my wife"
阿拉丁对她说："别害怕，你是我的妻子。"
"you were promised to me by your unjust father"
"你那不公正的父亲把你许配给了我"
"and no harm shall come to you"
"你不会受到任何伤害"
The Princess was too frightened to speak
公主吓得说不出话来
and she passed the most miserable night of her life
她度过了一生中最悲惨的一夜
although Aladdin lay down beside her and slept soundly
尽管阿拉丁躺在她旁边，睡得很香
At the appointed hour the genie fetched in the shivering bridegroom
到了约定的时间，妖怪把瑟瑟发抖的新郎叫了进来

he laid him in his place
他使他回到原处
and he transported the bed back to the palace
并把床运回了宫殿
Presently the Sultan came to wish his daughter good-morning
不久,苏丹来向女儿问早安
The unhappy Vizier's son jumped up and hid himself
不幸的宰相儿子跳了起来,躲了起来
and the Princess would not say a word
公主一句话也不说
and she was very sorrowful
她非常伤心
The Sultan sent her mother to her
苏丹派她的母亲来见她
"Why will you not speak to your father, child?"
"孩子,你为什么不跟你父亲说话?"
"What has happened?" she asked
"发生什么事了?"她问
The Princess sighed deeply
公主深深地叹了一口气
and at last she told her mother what had happened
最后她告诉了母亲发生的事情
she told her how the bed had been carried into some strange house
她告诉她床是如何被搬进一个陌生的房子的
and she told of what had happened in the house
她讲述了房子里发生的事情
Her mother did not believe her in the least
她的母亲根本不相信她
and she bade her to consider it an idle dream
她让她把这当作一场白日梦
The following night exactly the same thing happened
第二天晚上又发生了同样的事情

and the next morning the princess wouldn't speak either
第二天早上公主也不说话
on the Princess's refusal to speak, the Sultan threatened to cut off her head
公主拒绝说话,苏丹威胁要砍掉她的头
She then confessed all that had happened
然后她承认了发生的一切
and she bid him to ask the Vizier's son
她让他去问宰相的儿子
The Sultan told the Vizier to ask his son
苏丹让宰相去问儿子
and the Vizier's son told the truth
宰相的儿子说了实话
he added that he dearly loved the Princess
他补充说,他非常爱公主
"but I would rather die than go through another such fearful night"
"但我宁愿死也不愿再经历如此可怕的夜晚"
and he wished to be separated from her, which was granted
他希望和她分开,她的请求得到了批准
and then there was an end to the feasting and rejoicing
然后宴会和欢乐就结束了
then the three months were over
三个月过去了
Aladdin sent his mother to remind the Sultan of his promise
阿拉丁派他的母亲去提醒苏丹他的诺言
She stood in the same place as before
她站在原地
the Sultan had forgotten Aladdin
苏丹已经忘记了阿拉丁
but at once he remembered him again
但他马上又想起了他
and he asked for her to come to him
他请她到他身边来

On seeing her poverty the Sultan felt less inclined than ever to keep his word
看到她的贫困,苏丹比以往任何时候都更不愿意遵守诺言

and he asked his Vizier's advice
他向宰相征求意见

he counselled him to set a high value on the Princess
他劝他要高度重视公主

a price so high that no man alive could come afford her
价格如此之高,以至于没有一个男人能买得起她

The Sultan then turned to Aladdin's mother, saying:
然后苏丹转向阿拉丁的母亲说:

"Good woman, a Sultan must remember his promises"
"好女人,苏丹必须记住自己的诺言"

"and I will remember my promise"
"我会记得我的承诺"

"but your son must first send me forty basins of gold"
"但你儿子必须先给我送来四十盆金子"

"and the gold basins must be full of jewels"
"金盆里必须盛满珠宝"

"and they must be carried by forty black camels"
"它们必须由四十头黑骆驼驮运"

"and in front of each black camel there is to be a white camel"
"每只黑骆驼前面都会有一头白骆驼"

"and all the camels are to be splendidly dressed"
"所有的骆驼都要打扮得漂漂亮亮"

"Tell him that I await his answer"
"告诉他我在等他的答复"

The mother of Aladdin bowed low
阿拉丁的母亲深深鞠躬

and then she went home
然后她回家了

although she thought all was lost

尽管她以为一切都完了

She gave Aladdin the message
她给阿拉丁传达了信息

and she added, "He may wait long enough for your answer!"
她又补充道:"他可能要等很长时间才能听到你的答复!"

"Not so long as you think, mother," her son replied
儿子回答说:"妈妈,时间不会像你想的那么长。"

"I would do a great deal more than that for the Princess"
"我愿意为公主做更多的事情"

and he summoned the genie again
他再次召唤了精灵

and in a few moments the eighty camels arrived
不一会儿,八十头骆驼就到了

and they took up all space in the small house and garden
它们占据了小房子和花园的所有空间

Aladdin made the camels set out to the palace
阿拉丁让骆驼出发去宫殿

and the camels were followed by his mother
骆驼妈妈跟在后面

The camels were very richly dressed
骆驼穿得很华丽

and splendid jewels were on the girdles of the camels
骆驼的腰带上挂着华丽的珠宝

and everyone crowded around to see the camels
大家都围过来看骆驼

and they saw the basins of gold the camels carried on their backs
他们看到骆驼背上驮着金盆

They entered the palace of the Sultan
他们进入了苏丹的宫殿

and the camels kneeled before him in a semi circle
骆驼在他面前半圆形地跪下

and Aladdin's mother presented the camels to the Sultan

阿拉丁的母亲把骆驼送给苏丹

He hesitated no longer, but said:
他不再犹豫，而是说道：

"Good woman, return to your son"
"好女人，回到你儿子身边去吧"

"tell him that I wait for him with open arms"
"告诉他我张开双臂等他"

She lost no time in telling Aladdin
她立即告诉阿拉丁

and she bid him to make haste
她叫他赶紧

But Aladdin first called for the genie
但阿拉丁首先召唤了精灵

"I want a scented bath," he said
温情道："我想泡个香味澡。"

"and I want a horse more beautiful than the Sultan's"
"我想要一匹比苏丹的马更漂亮的马"

"and I want twenty servants to attend to me"
"我需要二十个仆人来照顾我"

"and I also want six beautifully dressed servants to wait on my mother"
"我还要六个衣着漂亮的仆人来侍奉我的母亲"

"and lastly, I want ten thousand pieces of gold in ten purses"
"最后，我要十个钱包里的一万块金币"

No sooner had he said what he wanted and it was done
他刚说完他想要什么，事情就完成了

Aladdin mounted his beautiful horse
阿拉丁骑上了他美丽的马

and he passed through the streets
他穿过街道

the servants cast gold into the crowd as they went
仆人们一边走，一边向人群中扔金子

Those who had played with him in his childhood knew him not

那些在他童年时和他一起玩耍的人都不认识他
he had grown very handsome
他变得非常英俊
When the Sultan saw him he came down from his throne
当苏丹看到他时,他从宝座上走下来
he embraced his new son-in-law with open arms
他张开双臂拥抱他的新女婿
and he led him into a hall where a feast was spread
他领他进入一个大厅,那里摆满了筵席。
he intended to marry him to the Princess that very day
他打算当天就让他和公主结婚
But Aladdin refused to marry straight away
但阿拉丁拒绝立即结婚
"first I must build a palace fit for the princess"
"首先我必须为公主建造一座宫殿"
and then he took his leave
然后他告辞了
Once home, he said to the genie:
回到家后,他对精灵说:
"Build me a palace of the finest marble"
"用最精美的大理石为我建造一座宫殿"
"set the palace with jasper, agate, and other precious stones"
"用碧玉、玛瑙和其他宝石镶嵌宫殿"
"In the middle of the palace you shall build me a large hall with a dome"
"你要在宫殿的中央为我建造一座有圆顶的大厅"
"the four walls of the hall will be of masses of gold and silver"
"大厅的四面墙壁将布满金银"
"and each wall will have six windows"
"每面墙都有六扇窗户"
"and the lattices of the windows will be set with precious jewels"
"窗户的窗棂上必镶着珍贵的宝石"

"but there must be one window that is not decorated"
"但必须有一扇窗户没有装饰"

"go see that it gets done!"
"去看看它是否完成了！"

The palace was finished by the next day
宫殿第二天就完工了

the genie carried him to the new palace
精灵把他带到了新宫殿

and he showed him how all his orders had been faithfully carried out
他向他展示了他的命令是如何得到忠实执行的

even a velvet carpet had been laid from Aladdin's palace to the Sultan's
甚至从阿拉丁的宫殿到苏丹的宫殿都铺上了天鹅绒地毯

Aladdin's mother then dressed herself carefully
阿拉丁的母亲小心翼翼地穿好衣服

and she walked to the palace with her servants
她和仆人一起走进宫殿

and Aladdin followed her on horseback
阿拉丁骑着马跟在她后面

The Sultan sent musicians with trumpets and cymbals to meet them
苏丹派出手持喇叭和钹的乐师去迎接他们

so the air resounded with music and cheers
空气中回荡着音乐和欢呼声

She was taken to the Princess, who saluted her
她被带到公主面前，公主向她致敬

and she treated her with great honour
她非常尊重地对待她

At night the Princess said good-bye to her father
晚上，公主与父亲告别

and she set out on the carpet for Aladdin's palace
她踏上前往阿拉丁宫殿的魔毯

his mother was at her side
他的母亲在她身边
and they were followed by their entourage of servants
后面跟着仆人
She was charmed at the sight of Aladdin
她一看到阿拉丁就被迷住了
and Aladdin ran to receive her into the palace
阿拉丁跑去迎接她进宫殿
"Princess," he said, "blame your beauty for my boldness"
"公主，"他说，"我的大胆都是因为你的美貌。"
"I hope I have not displeased you"
"我希望我没有让你不高兴"
she said she willingly obeyed her father in this matter
她说在这件事上她愿意听从父亲
because she had seen that he is handsome
因为她看到他很帅
After the wedding had taken place Aladdin led her into the hall
婚礼结束后，阿拉丁领着她走进大厅
a great feast was spread out in the hall
大厅里摆满了丰盛的宴席
and she supped with him
她和他共进晚餐
after eating they danced till midnight
吃完饭后他们跳舞直到午夜
The next day Aladdin invited the Sultan to see the palace
第二天，阿拉丁邀请苏丹参观宫殿
they entered the hall with the four-and-twenty windows
他们走进了有二十四扇窗户的大厅
the windows were decorated with rubies, diamonds, and emeralds
窗户上装饰着红宝石、钻石和绿宝石
he cried, "The palace is one of the wonders of the world!"
他大声喊道，"这座宫殿是世界奇迹之一！"

"There is only one thing that surprises me"
"只有一件事令我惊讶"
"Was it by accident that one window was left unfinished?"
"有一扇窗户没有完工是偶然的吗？"
"No, sir, it was done so by design," replied Aladdin
阿拉丁回答说："不是的，先生，这是故意设计的。"

"I wished your Majesty to have the glory of finishing this palace"
"我希望陛下能有幸完成这座宫殿。"
The Sultan was pleased to be given this honour
苏丹很高兴获此殊荣
and he sent for the best jewellers in the city
他派人把城里最好的珠宝商请来
He showed them the unfinished window
他向他们展示了未完成的窗户
and he bade them to decorate the window like the others
他命令他们像其他人一样装饰窗户
"Sir," replied their spokesman
"先生，"他们的发言人回答道
"we cannot find enough jewels"
"我们找不到足够的珠宝"
so the Sultan had his own jewels fetched
于是苏丹派人取来自己的珠宝
but those jewels were soon used up too
但这些珠宝很快就用完了
even after a month's time the work was not half done
即使过了一个月，工作还没有完成一半
Aladdin knew that their task was impossible
阿拉丁知道他们的任务是不可能完成的
he bade them to undo their work
他命令他们撤销他们的工作
and he bade them to carry the jewels back
他命令他们把珠宝带回去

the genie finished the window at his command
精灵按照他的命令完成了窗户
The Sultan was surprised to receive his jewels again
苏丹很惊讶再次收到他的珠宝
he visited Aladdin, who showed him the finished window
他拜访了阿拉丁，阿拉丁向他展示了完成的窗户
and the Sultan embraced his son in law
苏丹拥抱了他的女婿
meanwhile, the envious Vizier suspected the work of enchantment
与此同时，嫉妒的宰相怀疑这是魔法造成的
Aladdin had won the hearts of the people by his gentle manner
阿拉丁以他温和的举止赢得了人们的心
He was made captain of the Sultan's armies
他被任命为苏丹军队的队长
and he won several battles for his army
他为他的军队赢得了几场战斗
but he remained as modest and courteous as before
但他依然像以前一样谦虚有礼
in this way he lived in peace and content for several years
就这样他安居乐业地过了几年
But far away in Africa the magician remembered Aladdin
但远在非洲的魔术师记得阿拉丁
and by his magic arts he discovered Aladdin hadn't perished in the cave
他用魔法发现阿拉丁并没有死在山洞里
but instead of perishing, he had escaped and married the princess
但他没有死，而是逃了出来，并娶了公主
and now he was living in great honour and wealth
现在他过着富足而尊贵的生活
He knew that the poor tailor's son could only have accomplished this by means of the magic lamp
他知道这个可怜的裁缝儿子只有借助神灯才能做到这

一点

and he travelled night and day until he reached the city
他日夜兼程,终于到达了这座城市

he was bent on making sure of Aladdin's ruin
他一心要确保阿拉丁的毁灭

As he passed through the town he heard people talking
当他穿过小镇时,他听到人们在谈论

all they could talk about was the marvellous palace
他们谈论的都是那座宏伟的宫殿

"Forgive my ignorance," he asked
"请原谅我的无知,"他问道

"what is this palace you speak of?"
"您说的这个宫殿是什么?"

"Have you not heard of Prince Aladdin's palace?" was the reply
"你没听说过阿拉丁王子的宫殿吗?"

"the palace is one of the greatest wonders of the world"
"这座宫殿是世界上最伟大的奇迹之一"

"I will direct you to the palace, if you would like to see it"
"如果你想参观宫殿的话,我可以带你去那里。"

The magician thanked him for bringing him to the palace
魔术师感谢他把他带到宫殿

and having seen the palace, he knew that it had been built by the Genie of the Lamp
看到宫殿后,他知道这是灯神建造的

this made him half mad with rage
这让他气得半疯

He was determined to get hold of the magic lamp
他决心要得到神灯

and he was going to plunge Aladdin into the deepest poverty again
他又要让阿拉丁陷入极度贫困之中

Unluckily, Aladdin had gone on a hunting trip for eight days

不幸的是,阿拉丁出去打猎了八天
this gave the magician plenty of time
这给了魔术师充足的时间
He bought a dozen copper lamps
他买了一打铜灯
and he put the copper lamps into a basket
他把铜灯放进篮子里
and then he went to the palace
然后他去了宫殿
"New lamps for old lamps!" he exclaimed
"用新灯换旧灯!"他喊道
and he was followed by a jeering crowd
他身后跟着一群嘲笑他的人群
The Princess was sitting in the hall of four-and-twenty windows
公主坐在有二十四扇窗户的大厅里
she sent a servant to find out what the noise was about
她派了一个仆人去看看是什么声音
the servant came back laughing so much that the Princess scolded her
仆人笑着回来,公主责骂她
"Madam," replied the servant
"夫人。"仆人回答道。
"who can help but laughing when you see such a thing?"
"看到这种事谁能忍住不笑呢?"
"an old fool is offering to exchange fine new lamps for old lamps"
"一位老傻瓜愿意用漂亮的新灯来换旧灯"
Another servant, hearing this, spoke up
另一个仆人听到这话,说道
"There is an old lamp on the cornice which he can have"
"屋檐上有一盏旧灯,他可以拿走。"
this, of course, was the magic lamp
这当然是神灯

Aladdin had left the magic lamp there, as he could not take it with him
阿拉丁把神灯留在那里,因为他不能带走它。
The Princess didn't know know the lamp's value
公主不知道这盏灯的价值
laughingly, she bade the servant to exchange the magic lamp
她笑着吩咐仆人去换神灯
the servant took the lamp to the magician
仆人把灯拿给魔术师
"Give me a new lamp for this lamp," she said
她说:"给我换一盏新灯吧。"
He snatched the lamp and bade the servant to pick another lamp
他夺过灯,吩咐仆人拿另一盏灯
and the entire crowd jeered at the sight
人群中响起一片嘲笑声
but the magician cared little for the crowd
但魔术师并不关心观众
he left the crowd with the magic lamp he had set out to get
他带着他要拿的神灯离开了人群
and he went out of the city gates to a lonely place
他出了城门,到一个僻静的地方。
there he remained till nightfall
他一直呆到天黑
and at nightfall he pulled out the magic lamp and rubbed it
夜幕降临,他拿出神灯,擦了一下
The genie appeared to the magician
精灵出现在魔术师面前
and the magician made his command to the genie
魔术师向精灵发出命令
"carry me, the princess, and the palace to a lonely place in Africa"
"把我、公主和宫殿带到非洲一个荒凉的地方"
Next morning the Sultan looked out of the window toward Aladdin's palace

第二天早上，苏丹从窗外望向阿拉丁的宫殿
and he rubbed his eyes when he saw the palace was gone
当他看到宫殿不见了时，他揉了揉眼睛
He sent for the Vizier and asked what had become of the palace
他派人去请维齐尔，询问宫殿的情况
The Vizier looked out too, and was lost in astonishment
宰相也向外望去，惊呆了。
He again put the events down to enchantment
他再次把这些事件归因于魔法
and this time the Sultan believed him
这次苏丹相信了他
he sent thirty men on horseback to fetch Aladdin in chains
他派了三十个骑马的人去抓被锁链锁住的阿拉丁
They met him riding home
他们遇见他骑车回家
they bound him and forced him to go with them on foot
他们把他绑起来，强迫他步行跟他们走
The people, however, who loved him, followed them to the palace
然而，爱戴他的人们跟随他们来到宫殿
they would make sure that he came to no harm
他们会确保他不会受到伤害
He was carried before the Sultan
他被抬到苏丹面前
and the Sultan ordered the executioner to cut off his head
苏丹命令刽子手砍下他的头
The executioner made Aladdin kneel down before a block of wood
刽子手让阿拉丁跪在一块木头前
he bandaged his eyes so that he could not see
他用绷带包扎了眼睛，使他看不见
and he raised his scimitar to strike
他举起弯刀准备攻击

At that instant the Vizier saw the crowd had forced their way into the courtyard
就在这时，宰相看到人群已经涌进了庭院
they were scaling the walls to rescue Aladdin
他们正在爬墙去救阿拉丁
so he called to the executioner to halt
于是他叫刽子手停下来
The people, indeed, looked so threatening that the Sultan gave way
这些人确实看起来很有威胁性，苏丹让步了
and he ordered Aladdin to be unbound
他命令释放阿拉丁
he pardoned him in the sight of the crowd
他在众人面前赦免了他
Aladdin now begged to know what he had done
阿拉丁现在恳求知道他做了什么
"False wretch!" said the Sultan, "come thither"
"你这个骗子！"苏丹说道，"过来。"
he showed him from the window the place where his palace had stood
他从窗户向他展示了他的宫殿所在地
Aladdin was so amazed that he could not say a word
阿拉丁惊讶得说不出话来
"Where are my palace and my daughter?" demanded the Sultan
"我的宫殿和女儿在哪儿？"苏丹问道
"For the palace I am not so deeply concerned"
"我对宫殿并不太关心"
"but my daughter I must have"
"但我必须拥有我的女儿"
"and you must find her, or lose your head"
"你必须找到她，否则就会失去理智"
Aladdin begged to be granted forty days in which to find her
阿拉丁请求给予她四十天的时间去寻找她

he promised that if he failed he would return
他承诺如果失败了他会回来
and on his return he would suffer death at the Sultan's pleasure
回国后,苏丹将随意处死他
His prayer was granted by the Sultan
苏丹答应了他的请求
and he went forth sadly from the Sultan's presence
他悲伤地从苏丹面前走了出去
For three days he wandered about like a madman
三天里他像疯子一样四处游荡
he asked everyone what had become of his palace
他问每个人他的宫殿怎么样了
but they only laughed and pitied him
但他们只是笑着可怜他
He came to the banks of a river
他来到河岸边
he knelt down to say his prayers before throwing himself in
他跪下祈祷,然后投身其中
In so doing he rubbed the magic ring he still wore
这样一来,他就摩擦起自己仍戴着的魔法戒指
The genie he had seen in the cave appeared
他在山洞里见过的精灵出现了
and he asked him what his will was
他问他有什么愿望
"Save my life, genie," said Aladdin
阿拉丁说:"神灯,救救我吧。"
"bring my palace back"
"把我的宫殿带回来"
"That is not in my power," said the genie
"这不在我的掌控之中,"精灵说
"I am only the Slave of the Ring"
"我只是魔戒的奴隶"
"you must ask him for the magic lamp"

"你必须向他要魔灯"
"that might be true," said Aladdin
阿拉丁说:"那可能是真的。"
"but thou canst take me to the palace"
"但你可以带我去宫殿"
"set me down under my dear wife's window"
"把我放在我亲爱的妻子的窗户下面"
He at once found himself in Africa
他立刻发现自己身处非洲
he was under the window of the Princess
他在公主的窗户下面
and he fell asleep out of sheer weariness
他因为极度疲倦而睡着了
He was awakened by the singing of the birds
他被鸟儿的歌声吵醒了
and his heart was lighter than it was before
他的心情也比以前轻松多了
He saw that all his misfortunes were due to the loss of the magic lamp
他意识到自己所有的不幸都是因为丢失了神灯
and he vainly wondered who had robbed him of his magic lamp
他徒劳地想知道是谁抢走了他的神灯
That morning the Princess rose earlier than she normally
那天早上,公主起得比平时早
once a day she was forced to endure the magicians company
每天她都被迫忍受魔术师的陪伴
She, however, treated him very harshly
然而,她却对他非常严厉
so he dared not live with her in the palace
所以他不敢和她一起住在宫里
As she was dressing, one of her women looked out and saw Aladdin
当她穿衣服的时候,她的一个女仆向外看,看到了阿

拉丁

The Princess ran and opened the window
公主跑去打开窗户

at the noise she made Aladdin looked up
听到她发出的声音,阿拉丁抬起头来

She called to him to come to her
她叫他过来

it was a great joy for the lovers to see each other again
这对恋人再次相见感到非常高兴

After he had kissed her Aladdin said:
阿拉丁亲吻了她之后说道:

"**I beg of you, Princess, in God's name**"
"我恳求你,公主,以上帝的名义"

"**before we speak of anything else**"
"在我们谈论其他事情之前"

"**for your own sake and mine**"
"为了你和我"

"**tell me what has become of the old lamp**"
"告诉我这盏旧灯怎么样了"

"**I left the lamp on the cornice in the hall of four-and-twenty windows**"
"我把灯放在了有二十四个窗户的大厅的檐口上"

"**Alas!**" she said, "**I am the innocent cause of our sorrows**"
"唉!"她说,"我才是我们痛苦的罪魁祸首。"

and she told him of the exchange of the magic lamp
她告诉他交换神灯的事

"**Now I know,**" **cried Aladdin**
阿拉丁喊道:"现在我知道了。"

"**we have to thank the magician for this!**"
"这我们要感谢魔术师!"

"**Where is the magic lamp?**"
"魔灯在哪儿?"

"**He carries the lamp about with him,**" **said the Princess**
"他随身带着灯,"公主说。

"I know he carries the lamp with him"
"我知道他随身带着灯"

"because he pulled the lamp out of his breast pocket to show me"
"因为他从胸前的口袋里掏出了灯给我看"

"and he wishes me to break my faith with you and marry him"
"他希望我背弃对你的忠诚,嫁给他"

"and he said you were beheaded by my father's command"
"他说你是按照我父亲的命令被斩首的"

"He is always speaking ill of you"
"他总是说你的坏话"

"but I only reply with my tears"
"但我只用眼泪来回答"

"If I can persist, I doubt not"
"如果我能坚持下去,我就不会怀疑"

"but he will use violence"
"但他会使用暴力"

Aladdin comforted his wife
阿拉丁安慰他的妻子

and he left her for a while
他离开了她一段时间

He changed clothes with the first person he met in town
他和在城里遇到的第一个人换了衣服

and having bought a certain powder, he returned to the Princess
他买了一些粉末,然后回到公主那里

the Princess let him in by a little side door
公主让他从一扇小侧门进来

"Put on your most beautiful dress," he said to her
他对她说:"穿上你最漂亮的裙子。"

"receive the magician with smiles today"
"今天用微笑迎接魔术师"

"lead him to believe that you have forgotten me"

"让他相信你已经忘记我了"
"Invite him to sup with you"
"请他和你一起吃饭"
"and tell him you wish to taste the wine of his country"
"并告诉他你想尝尝他国家的葡萄酒"
"He will be gone for some time"
"他会离开一段时间"
"while he is gone I will tell you what to do"
"他走后我会告诉你该怎么做"
She listened carefully to Aladdin
她认真听着阿拉丁
and when he left she arrayed herself beautifully
当他离开时,她打扮得漂漂亮亮
she hadn't dressed like this since she had left her city
自从离开这座城市后,她就没有穿过这样的衣服
She put on a girdle and head-dress of diamonds
她戴上了钻石腰带和头饰
she was more beautiful than ever
她比以前更美丽
and she received the magician with a smile
她微笑着迎接魔术师
"I have made up my mind that Aladdin is dead"
"我已经认定阿拉丁已经死了"
"my tears will not bring him back to me"
"我的眼泪无法让他回到我身边"
"so I am resolved to mourn no more"
"所以我决定不再悲伤"
"therefore I invite you to sup with me"
"因此我邀请你和我一起吃饭"
"but I am tired of the wines we have"
"但我厌倦了我们的葡萄酒"
"I would like to taste the wines of Africa"
"我想品尝非洲的葡萄酒"
The magician ran to his cellar

魔术师跑到他的地窖里
and the Princess put the powder Aladdin had given her in her cup
公主把阿拉丁给她的粉末放进了她的杯子里
When he returned she asked him to drink to her health
当他回来时,她请他为她的健康干杯
and she handed him her cup in exchange for his
她把杯子递给他,作为交换
this was done as a sign to show she was reconciled to him
这样做是为了表明她已经和他和好了
Before drinking the magician made her a speech
喝酒之前,魔术师对她发表了演讲
he wanted to praise her beauty
他想赞美她的美丽
but the Princess cut him short
但公主打断了他的话
"Let us drink first"
"我们先喝酒吧"
"and you shall say what you will afterwards"
"然后你就可以随心所欲地说了"
She set her cup to her lips and kept it there
她把杯子放到唇边,
the magician drained his cup to the dregs
魔术师喝光了杯子里的酒
and upon finishing his drink he fell back lifeless
喝完酒他就倒地不起了
The Princess then opened the door to Aladdin
公主为阿拉丁打开了门
and she flung her arms round his neck
她张开双臂搂住他的脖子
but Aladdin asked her to leave him
但阿拉丁要求她离开他
there was still more to be done
还有更多工作要做

He then went to the dead magician
然后他走向死去的魔术师
and he took the lamp out of his vest
他从背心里拿出灯
he bade the genie to carry the palace back
他命令精灵把宫殿带回来
the Princess in her chamber only felt two little shocks
公主在房间里只感觉到了两次轻微的震动
in little time she was at home again
没过多久她就回到家了
The Sultan was sitting on his balcony
苏丹坐在阳台上
he was mourning for his lost daughter
他正在哀悼他失去的女儿
he looked up and had to rub his eyes again
他抬起头，又不得不揉了揉眼睛
the palace stood there as it had before
宫殿依然矗立在那里
He hastened over to the palace to see his daughter
他赶紧去宫殿看望女儿
Aladdin received him in the hall of the palace
阿拉丁在宫殿的大厅里接待了他
and the princess was at his side
公主就在他身边
Aladdin told him what had happened
阿拉丁告诉他发生的事情
and he showed him the dead body of the magician
他向他展示了魔术师的尸体
so that the Sultan would believe him
以便苏丹相信他
A ten days' feast was proclaimed
宣布举行十天的盛宴
and it seemed as if Aladdin might now live the rest of his life in peace

看来阿拉丁现在可以安度余生了
but his life was not to be as peaceful as he had hoped
但他的生活并不像他希望的那样平静
The African magician had a younger brother
这位非洲魔术师有一个弟弟
he was maybe even more wicked and cunning than his brother
他可能比他哥哥更邪恶、更狡猾
He travelled to Aladdin to avenge his brother's death
他去阿拉丁为弟弟报仇
he went to visit a pious woman called Fatima
他去拜访一位名叫法蒂玛的虔诚妇女
he thought she might be of use to him
他认为她可能对他有用
He entered her cell and put a dagger to her breast
他进入她的牢房,用匕首抵住她的胸口
then he told her to rise and do his bidding
然后他叫她起来,听从他的命令
and if she didn't he said he would kill her
如果她不这样做,他说他会杀了她
He changed his clothes with her
他和她换衣服
and he coloured his face like hers
他的脸色跟她的一样
he put on her veil so that he looked just like her
他戴上她的面纱,这样他看起来就和她一模一样
and finally he murdered her despite her compliance
最后他不顾她的顺从,将她杀死
so that she could tell no tales
这样她就没法说闲话了
Then he went towards the palace of Aladdin
然后他走向阿拉丁的宫殿
all the people thought he was the holy woman
所有人都以为他是圣女

they gathered round him to kiss his hands
他们围着他,亲吻他的手
and they begged for his blessing
他们祈求他的祝福
When he got to the palace there was a great commotion around him
当他到达宫殿时,周围一片喧闹
the princess wanted to know what all the noise was about
公主想知道这些噪音是怎么回事
so she bade her servant to look out of the window
于是她吩咐仆人往窗外看
and her servant asked what the noise was all about
仆人问她听到了什么声音
she found out it was the holy woman causing the commotion
她发现是圣女引起了骚动
she was curing people of their ailments by touching them
她通过触摸来治愈人们的疾病
the Princess had long desired to see Fatima
公主一直渴望见到法蒂玛
so she got her servant to ask her into the palace
于是她让仆人请她进宫
and the false Fatima accepted the offer into the palace
假法蒂玛接受了邀请,进入宫殿
the magician offered up a prayer for her health and prosperity
魔术师为她的健康和繁荣祈祷
the Princess made him sit by her
公主让他坐在她旁边
and she begged him to stay with her
她恳求他留下来陪她
The false Fatima wished for nothing better
假法蒂玛别无所求
and she consented to the princess' wish
她答应了公主的愿望

but he kept his veil down
但他没有戴面纱

because he knew that he would be discovered otherwise
因为他知道如果不这样做的话，他就会被发现

The Princess showed him the hall
公主带他参观了大厅

and she asked him what he thought of the hall
她问他觉得大厅怎么样

"It is a truly beautiful hall," said the false Fatima
"这真是一座美丽的大厅，"假法蒂玛说道。

"but in my mind your palace still wants one thing"
"但在我看来你的宫殿仍然想要一件事"

"And what is it that my palace is missing?" asked the Princess
"我的宫殿里少了什么东西？"公主问

"If only a Roc's egg were hung up from the middle of this dome"
"如果这座穹顶的中央能挂一颗大鹏鸟蛋就好了"

"then your palace would be the wonder of the world," he said
"那么你的宫殿将成为世界奇迹，"他说

After this the Princess could think of nothing but the Roc's egg
此后，公主一心只想着大鹏鸟的蛋

when Aladdin returned from hunting he found her in a very ill humour
阿拉丁打猎回来后发现她心情很不好

He begged to know what was amiss
他恳求知道发生了什么事

and she told him what had spoiled her pleasure
她告诉他是什么让她不开心

"I'm made miserable for the want of a Roc's egg"
"我因为缺少一只大鹏鸟的蛋而痛苦不堪"

"If that is all you want you shall soon be happy," replied Aladdin

阿拉丁回答说:"如果这就是你想要的,你很快就会幸福的。"

he left her and rubbed the lamp
他离开了她,擦了擦灯

when the genie appeared he commanded him to bring a Roc's egg
当精灵出现时,他命令他带一颗大鹏鸟蛋

The genie gave such a loud and terrible shriek that the hall shook
妖怪发出一声可怕的尖叫,大厅都震动了

"Wretch!" he cried, "is it not enough that I have done everything for you?"
"可怜虫!"他喊道,"我为你做的一切还不够吗?"

"but now you command me to bring my master"
"但现在你命令我带我的主人来"

"and you want me to hang him up in the midst of this dome"
"你想让我把他吊在这座穹顶中央吗?"

"You and your wife and your palace deserve to be burnt to ashes"
"你和你的妻子以及你的宫殿都应该被烧成灰烬"

"but this request does not come from you"
"但这个请求不是你提出的"

"the demand comes from the brother of the magician"
"这个要求来自魔术师的兄弟"

"the magician whom you have destroyed"
"你毁掉的魔术师"

"He is now in your palace disguised as the holy woman"
"他现在在你的宫殿里,伪装成圣女。"

"the real holy woman he has already murdered"
"他已经谋杀了真正的圣女"

"it was him who put that wish into your wife's head"
"是他把这个愿望植入了你妻子的脑海里"

"Take care of yourself, for he means to kill you"

"照顾好自己,因为他想杀你"
upon saying this, the genie disappeared
说完这句话,妖怪就消失了

Aladdin went back to the Princess
阿拉丁回到公主身边

he told her that his head ached
他告诉她他的头很痛

so she requested the holy Fatima to be fetched
于是她请求将圣法蒂玛带来

she could lay her hands on his head
她可以把手放在他的头上

and his headache would be cured by her powers
他的头痛就会被她的力量治愈

when the magician came near Aladdin seized his dagger
当魔术师走近时,阿拉丁抓起了他的匕首

and he pierced him in the heart
刺穿了他的心

"What have you done?" cried the Princess
"你做了什么?"公主大叫

"You have killed the holy woman!"
"你害死了圣女!"

"It is not so," replied Aladdin
阿拉丁回答:"不是这样的。"

"I have killed a wicked magician"
"我杀了一个邪恶的魔术师"

and he told her of how she had been deceived
他告诉她她是如何被欺骗的

After this Aladdin and his wife lived in peace
从此以后阿拉丁和他的妻子过上了平静的生活。

He succeeded the Sultan when he died
苏丹去世后,他继承了苏丹的王位

he reigned over the kingdom for many years
他统治这个王国很多年

and he left behind him a long lineage of kings

他留下了一代又一代的国王

The End
结束

www.ingramcontent.com/pod-product-compliance
Lightning Source LLC
Chambersburg PA
CBHW012010090526
44590CB00026B/3951